A Short Sketch of the Early History of the Town and Island of Bombay

A SHORT SKETCH

OF THE

EARLY HISTORY

OF THE

TOWN & ISLAND OF BOMBAY.

HINDU PERIOD.

BY

PURUSHOTTAM BALKRISHNA JOSHI,

Fellow of the Bombay University,
Author of Padyasudha, Anandodgdr and other Marathi Poems.

————◆◆◆————

PUBLISHED AT THE "TIMES OF INDIA" PRESS

1902.

CONTENTS.

PREFACE.

THE following short sketch was written at the suggestion of S. M. Edwardes, Esq., I.C.S., about a year ago, and a portion of it has appeared in that officer's Census Report, Volume X, Part IV, History of Bombay. But as Mr. Edwardes has utilized only as much portion of it as was needful for the purposes of his Census Report, and as copies of the Census Report containing the History of Bombay are not available for the general public, at the suggestion of certain friends, it is considered advisable to publish the sketch in its present shape. It is mostly intended for private circulation, and the writer has no desire to make any profits out of the sale-proceeds of the book.

Hitherto, most of the writers of the history of Bombay have confined their labours to describing the events that occurred from the date of the occupation and possession of this island, by the Portuguese and the British Governments. The history prior to these periods was considered a sealed letter. The reason for this is not far to seek. Most of these writers, being Europeans or foreigners, had no direct knowledge of, or access to, the rare and valuable materials and information that could be gathered from the descendants of the followers of Bhimadev or from other ancient families. But, when we find that even the story of the advent of Bhima Raja, was, in certain quarters, disbelieved or considered as a myth, we can easily account for the apathy shown by these writers, in this direction.

Since the following sketch was written, some interesting and valuable information has come to hand from different sources regarding Bhima Raja and his successors, the most important piece of information being the discovery of the site of the ancient city of Pratappur in the village of Parjapur near Marol. According to Marathi accounts and local traditions, it is believed that Pratapdev built a new city near Marol, in Salsette, and called it Pratappur after his own name. With a view to obtaining some traces of this ancient city near Marol, Mr. S. M. Edwardes and the writer of this sketch went on the 29th of December, 1901, to Parjapur, and there, after a most careful and lengthy search, were discovered three images of Hindu goddesses (buried under ground), and traces of about six temples and an equal number of ponds. A full account of this has already appeared in the *Times of India* of the 16th of April, 1902.*

The identity of the Bhima Raja of Bombay is still in dispute. Dr. G. DaCunha and others hold that he was a Gujarat monarch, and in his "Origin of Bombay," Dr. Cunha has tried to identify him with the Bhimadev of the Chalukya dynasty, who flourished at Anahilwada about the year 1024, and who, on his being defeated by the notorious Mahomed of Ghazni, fled to Baglan. But, this theory is not borne out by any authentic historical evidence ; and how the learned writer has failed in this attempt has been clearly shown at pages 15-18 of this treatise. On the other hand, the language, dress, names and localities of family deities, names and surnames, and traditions† and records of the followers of the Bhima

---

* *Vide* Appendix B.

† A. M. T. Jackson, Esq., M.A., I.C.S., has given special attention to the study of the available literature and traditions about Bhima Raja, and his special proficiency in Sanskrit and Marathi has afforded him great facilities in his investigations. A special interest, therefore, attaches to his opinion on this subject. In a letter dated London, 3rd July, 1901, Mr. Jackson says :—"Your information about Bhima Raja is interesting and valuable. The traditions of the Madhyandina Brahmans of Thana are all in favour of a Deccan home and confirm the connection of Bhima Raja with Mungi Paithan."

Raja of Bombay all tend to prove, that he and his followers, originally belonged to the Dekkan, and that they came to the North Konkan, by the way of Gujarat. I do not claim finality for the views expressed by me on this point. I am open to correction, and any suggestions or fresh evidence in support of, or against, the views expressed in this treatise will be welcome. We have set the ball in motion; and the field for fresh research and final success is wide open for any one who wishes to work and win the laurels.

P. B. JOSHI.

BOMBAY, 1st June 1902.

EARLY HISTORY

OF THE

TOWN & ISLAND OF BOMBAY.

HINDU PERIOD.

CHAPTER I.

OF the early history of the town and island of Bombay very little is known. None of the writers, who have written works on Bombay, has attempted to give to the public a connected narrative of the history of the island from the earliest times. This is, to some extent, due to want of materials, as some of these which are now available were not then known or procurable; and even now, one in search of materials for writing the early history of the Konkan or of Bombay (the early history of Bombay being closely connected with that of the Northern Konkan), must content himself with what little information he can gather from old documents, coins, inscriptions in cave-temples, copperplate grants, patents, and similar other antiquarian relics.

The earliest mention (by European writers) of the town and island of Bombay appears to have been by Ptolemy, (A.D. 150), who calls the islands of Bombay and Salsette under the name of *Heptanesia*, or the Seven Islands. Ptolemy calls the Konkan "Ariaka," and according to this writer, the whole of the province of Ariaka was under the sovereignty of the lord of Tagar. By the early Sanskrit writers of the Puranic period the Konkan is called "Aparanta" or "Aparantak," and the name Ariaka given by Ptolemy can, thus, be easily identified with the Sanskrit name "Aparantaka." From the rock inscriptions of the famous King Asoka which are now found at Girnar in Kathiawar, at Khalsi in the Himalayas, and at Shahabazgarhi in the Afghan territory, we find that in the middle of the third century before Christ, Asoka sent his ministers of the religion of Buddha, to Rastikas, Pethanikas, and Aparantas.[1] In the Mahavanso[2] (a Ceylonese chronicle), it is stated that the Buddhist high-priest, Moggaliputto, under the direction of King Asoka, sent preachers of Buddhism to Maharatta, Aparanta and Banavasi. King Asoka was the grandson of the celebrated Chandragupta

Side notes: Ptolemy's Heptanesia.   The Mauryas.

[1] Inscriptions of Ashoka, Vol. II, 84.
[2] Turnour's Mahavanso, pp. 71—73.

of Pataliputra, who founded the Maurya dynasty ; and.
he flourished between B.C. 213 and 229. In all
likelihood, the province of Aparantaka, was under the
sway of King Asoka, and this belief is strengthened
by the fact that a fragment of the eighth Edict of
King Asoka was found at Supara, which was then
the capital of the Northern Konkan.

The Nasik cave inscriptions, throw some light, as to
the kings who ruled over the province of Aparantaka,
or who are described as lords of Apa-
**The Satava-
hanas or
Andhra-
bhrltyas.** ranta and other provinces. Thus, in
the longest of the four inscriptions
occurring in the cave temple at one
extremity of the hill at Nasik, we are told that in the
19th year of the reign of King Pulumayi, the cave was
constructed and dedicated for the use of the Buddhist
saints and mendicants by Gotami, mother of King
Gotamiputra Satakarni.[1] The King Gotamiputra
is described as being a king of kings, and ruler of
Asika, Asmak, Mulaka, Surashtra (Kathiawar),
Aparanta, Kukura, Anupa (province to the north
of Vindhya), Vidarbha (the Berars), and Akravanti
(Malwa). He belonged to the Satavāhan dynasty,
and is said to have destroyed the Sakas, Yavanas
and Palhavas, and re-established the glory of
the Satavāhna dynasty.[2] The Yavanas referred to

---

[1] *Bombay Gazetteer*, Vol. I, Part II, 149.

[2] *Bombay Gazetteer*, Nasik, Vol. XVI ; also *Bombay Gazetteer*, Vol. I,
Part II, 150.

above, are considered by Dr. Bhandarkar as the Bactrian Greeks,[1] and the probable date of the reign of King Gotamiputra is about 133—154 A.D.[2] That the Northern Konkan was under the rule of the Satavahanás is best evidenced by the find of a silver coin in the Stupa discovered at Sopara, in the year 1882, by Sir James Campbell and Pandit Bhagwanlal Indraji. This coin, which belongs to the dynasty of the Satavahanás, bears the following inscription :— " Ranno Gotamiputasa, Siri Yanna Satakanisa," *i.e.*, this coin belongs to King Gotamiputra Shri Yajna Satakarni[3]. These Satavahanás are the same as the Andhrabhrityas of the Hindu Purans, and probably identical with the Salivahanás of the local tradition.

Two hoards of silver coins, bearing the legend " The illustrious Krishna Raja, the great lord meditating at the feet of his mother and father," were found, one in the island of Bombay, and the other in Salsette. From the above, it is inferred that the early Rashtrakuta King Krishna (A.D. 375—400), whose coins have also been found at Karhad

The Kalachuris and Mauryas. coins have also been found at Karhad in Satara and at Nasik, also held sway over the Northern Konkan.[4] Dr. Fleet disputes, and we think rightly, the correctness of the tendency to refer these coins to an early Rashtrakuta king, and he believes that they belong

---

[1] Bhandarkar's Dekkhan, in *Bombay Gazetteer*, Vol. I, Part II, 149-50.
[2] *Ibid*, p. 166.
[3] *Bombay. Gazetteer*, Thana, Vol. XIV, 332.
[4] Cunningham's Arch. Surv., Report IX, 30.

to King Krishnaraja of the Kalachuri dynasty. [1] How long the Kalachuris ruled over the Northern Konkan it is not definitely known ; but we find that in the 6th century of the Christian era, kings of the Maurya dynasty were *again* ruling in the Konkan. Kirtivarman (I) of the Chalukya dynasty, who flourished about 567—591 A.D., is said to have invaded the Northern Konkan and defeated the Mauryas, [2] who appear to have been the paramount power of the Konkan till the middle of the 6th century. Pulakeshi, son of Kirtivarman, not only again invaded the

The Chalu-kyas. Konkan, but conquered it, and thus put an end to the sovereignty of the Mauryas in the Northern Konkan. He directed his General, Chand Danda, to take with him hundreds of ships and to attack Puri, the capital of the Mauryas, which was in such a flourishing condition, that it was called the goddess of the fortunes of the western ocean. [3] This Pulakeshi (II) was the most powerful of the Chalukya kings, and had brought under subjection the kings of Lata, Malwa, Gurjar, Kanoj and Banavasi. It was during his reign (611—640 A.D.), that the celebrated Chinese traveller, Hwan Thsang, visited the Maharashtra. [4]

Although Pulakeshi captured the most important towns of Puri and Banavasi, he does not appear to have

[1] Fleet's Dynasties of the Kanarese Districts, ch. I, p. 296.
[2] Ind. Ant., Vol. VIII, 244.
[3] Burgess' Arch. Surv., Report III, 26.
[4] Ind. Ant., Vol. VII, 290.

made either of them the capital of his vast dominions. The town of Puri, as has been stated before, was the capital of the kingdom of the Maurya rulers of the Konkan, and as will be shown hereafter, it was also the capital of the Silahara kings. The site of this place, has not yet been definitely identified. Professor Wilson holds that it was at Thana ; Sir James Campbell thinks that it might be the *Moreh* Bunder to the north-east end of Gharapuri or Elephanta ; and the late Rev. A. K. Nairne suggested that it might be the island of Gharapuri in the Bombay harbour. Mr. Cousens, in his recent archæological report, asserts that it must be the island of Elephanta in the Bombay harbour.[1]

How ·long the Chalukyas were in possession of the Konkan there are no means of knowing definitely, but in all likelihood they were the masters of this country till the rise of the Silaharas in A.D. 810.

Twenty Silahara kings ruled in the North Konkan from about 810 to 1260 A.D. As has already been stated, the capital of their kingdom was Puri, the modern island of Gharapuri in the Bombay harbour, and their other places of importance were Hanyaman (Sanjan), Shri Sthának (Thana), Chaul, Lonad, and Uran. They .called themselves Tagarpura-parameshwar, or the

The Silaharas.

---

1 *Vide* " Bombay Gazette " of January 5th, 1901.

lords of the excellent city of Tagarpura, and claimed descent from Jimutvahan.[1]

Kapardi was the first Silahara king of the North Konkan (Thana branch), but nothing special is known of him. He was succeeded by his son, Pulakeshi, and, in an inscription in Kanheri Cave, No. 78, he is described as the Governor of Mangulpuri in the Konkan, and as the humble servant of the Rashtra-kuta King Amoghavarsha. From the above it can be inferred that the Silaharas were subordinate to the Rashtrakutas. Of Kapardi (II), and Papuvanna, the 3rd and 4th Silahara kings, we have nothing of importance to narrate, except that from two inscriptions in the Kanheri Caves, Nos. 10 and 78, we learn that Kapardi (II) was also a subordinate of the Rashtra-kutas. Jhanjha, the 5th king, is mentioned by the Arab historian Masudi, as ruling over Saimur (Chaul) in 916 A.D.[2] Aparajita, the 8th king, appears to have shaken off the yoke of the Rashtrakutas, for it appears from a copperplate grant, dated 997 A.D., and found at Bher in Bhiwandi, that, during the reign of this king, the Rashtrakuta overlord, Kakkal, was defeated and slain by the Chalukya king Tailapa, and that Aparajita became independent.[3] In a copperplate grant, dated 1097 A.D., Arikesari, the 10th king, is described as

---

[1] An excellent account of how Jimutvahan, by his self-sacrifice, saved his tribe from the oppression of Garud or Wasuki is given in the Sanskrit drama called *Nágánand*.

[2] *Bombay Gazetteer*, Vol. I, Part II, 17.

[3] *Bombay Gazetteer*, Vol. I, Part II, 18.

lord of 1,400 villages in the Konkan, and mention is made of Puri, Shristhanak and Hanyaman as principal cities.[1] The 11th king was Chhittaraj, who is styled in a copperplate grant dated 1025 A.D. as the ruler of 1,400 Konkan villages, the chief of which were Puri and Hanyaman (Sanjan).[2] Mallikarjuna, the 17th Silahara king, was a powerful ruler, who had assumed the title of *Raja-pitamaha*, or the grand-father of kings. It is stated that, on one occasion, a bard of the king Mallikarjuna, went to the Court of Kumarpal, the king of Gujarat, and there sang certain verses in which Mallikarjuna was styled the grand-father of kings. This, so aroused the anger of Kumarpal, that, he ordered his General, Ambada, to invade the country of Mallikarjuna. Mallikarjuna opposed him, and in the battle which followed, Ambada was defeated, and forced to return to Gujarat. Kumarpal equipped a larger force, and again sent his General against Mallikarjuna. This time Ambada was successful. Mallikarjuna was defeated and slain, and Ambada, went in triumph to Anahilpura, the capital of his sovereign.

Soma or Someshwar was the last King of the Silahara dynasty who ruled over the Konkan, but like King Mallikarjuna he was an unlucky Sovereign. In the year 1260 A.D., Mahadev, King of Devagiri, invaded

The Yadavas of Devagiri.

---

[1] *Bombay Gazetteer*, Vol. I, Part II, 18.
[2] Ind. Ant., V, 276.

the Konkan with a large army in which there was a large number of elephants. In the battle which followed, Someshwar was defeated. So he took shelter in his ships, and met with his death, probably, by being drowned in the sea. [1]

After the defeat and death of Someshwar, the province of Northern Konkan was annexed to the kingdom of Devagiri, and hereafter, it appears to have been governed by a Viceroy appointed by the Devagiri kings. Mahadev died about the year 1271, and was succeeded by Ramadev as king of Devagiri. According to Dr. Fleet, (Dynasties of the Kanarese Districts, p. 529), in the year 1272 A.D., Mahapradhana (Chief Minister) Achyuta Nayaka was governing the province of Sasati (Salsette), as Viceroy of King Ramadev of Devagiri; and from one of the Thana copperplates published by Mr. Wathen, we find that in the year *shaka* 1212, *i.e.*, A.D. 1290, a Brahman, named Krishna, belonging to the Bharadwaja gotra, was the Viceroy of King Ramadev for the whole of the Konkan. In the year 1294 A.D. Alla-ud-din Khilji of Delhi invaded Devagiri. Ramadev, who did not expect such a sudden attack, was quite

---

[1] Hemadri, the celebrated Minister of Mahadev and Ramadev, in his Raja-prashasti, verse 17, says :—" यदीय गंध द्विप गंड पाली । निष्च्युत दानाम्बु तरंगिणीषु ॥ सोमः समुद्रेव पेशलोऽपि । ममजसैन्यैः सह कुंकुणेशः ॥ १७ ॥ *i.e.*, Soma, the lord of the Konkan, though expert in swimming in the sea, was, along with his army, drowned in the rivers formed by the humour falling from the temples of the intoxicated elephants of King Mahadev.

unprepared to oppose the Musalman force. He,
however, hurriedly collected about 4,000 men, and
opposed the advance of Alla-ud-din. In the battle which
followed, Ramadev, and his son, Shankar, were defeated, and Ramadev was obliged to sue for peace, on
payment of an annual tribute to the Emperor of Delhi.[1]
Ramadev had two sons, Shankardev and Bhimadev
or Bimbadev.

After the defeat of King Ramadev, Bimba or Bhimadev appears to have established himself as the king
or ruler of the Northern Konkan. From old Maratha
and Persian records, now in the possession of the
family of the late Sirdesai of Malad (and some of
which are *at present* in our possession), we learn that
King Bimbadev, after firmly establishing his power in
the Northern Konkan, made Mahi-Mahim (Bombay-
Mahim) the capital of his kingdom, and divided the
country into 15 mahals or districts, comprising in all
1,624 villages. According to the Bimbakhyana, King
Bimbadev came to the Konkan by the way of Anahilwada in the year 1216 *shaka*, that is, 1294 A.D.[2] Finding the island of Mahim (Bombay), almost uninhabited,
he gave orders for populating it, and was so much
pleased with the charming scenery of the island, that
he caused a royal palace and several houses to be

---

[1] *Bombay Gazetteer*, Vol. I, Part II, 251; also Elliot's History of
India, Vol. VII, p. 77.

[2] It should be noted that this year (1216) exactly corresponds with
the year in which Alla-ud-din invaded Devagiri and defeated Ramadev—
vide Bimbakhyana, p. 108.

built there, for the accommodation of various royal and other guests and persons, who came with him to the Konkan, through the fear of the Musalman invaders of Devagiri and Anahilwada.[1] King Bimbadev, is said to have brought with him, from Paithan, nine families of Yajurvedi Brahmans of the Madhyándina Shákha ; and from Paithan, Champaner, and other places 66 other families, *i.e.*, 27 kulas, or families of the Soma-vanshis, 12 families of the Suryavanshis, 9 of Shesha-vanshis, 5 families of Panchals, 7 of Kunbis or Agris, 1 family of Dasa-Lad, 1 of Visa-Lad, 1 of Moda, 1 of Dasa Moda, and 1 family of Visa Moda.[2]

The Bimbakhyana, an old Marathi work, gives an account of the advent of Bimbashah to the North Konkan, and of the people, who accompanied him. But, most of the dates, are inaccurate, and, in some places the statements are so very conflicting, that, unless they are corroborated by some other independent evidence, they can, hardly, be accepted as correct or reliable.

Let us, therefore, see what informátion we can gather from other sources. From a Persian firman issued by Nawab Chandakhan, Subha of the province of Damaun, and dated 901 A.H., *i.e.*, 1495 A.D., we learn that Bimbashah, hearing of the defeat of his father, Ramadev of Devagiri, by Alla-ud-din, fled with the Ra-jaguru Purushottam Punt Kavle, and eleven Umravs,

---

[1] Bimbakhyana, p. 108.
[2] Bimbakhyana, pp. 54-55.

by sea-shore, and, took possession of the fort of Parnera,
and of Bardi, Sanjan, Damaun, Shirgaon, &c.   Thus,
he got the territory from Parner to Astagar.   He came
to Mahi-Mahim (Bombay), and, divided the country
into 12 parts, and, gave the province of Malad and
some villages from the province of Pahad, to the Raja-
guru Kavle.[1]   In the Bimbakhyana it is stated that
the king gave the village of Pahad to the Raja-purohit
Kavle, and the village of Paspavli (Palsavli), to the
Senadhipati and Kulguru Gangadharpant Nayak.
This Nayak family appears to have been in high favour
with the Devagiri kings, for we find (from Dr. Fleet's
Kanarese Dynasties, p. 529) that in the year 1272 A.D.
Mahapradhan Achyut Nayak was governing the
province of Salsette as the Viceroy of Ramadev.

From a Persian patent, bearing the seal of Mahomed Dalil, Dewan of Sultan Alla-ud-din of Bedar, and
dated the first year of the accession to the throne,
that is, about the year 1436 A.D., we find that, "In
the Shalivahan era 1212 (1290 A.D.) Raja Bimbashah
having taken the ownership and possession of the
country from the hands of Karsan, kept it for himself.

---

[1] The descendants of this Raja-guru Kavle are still at Malad as
Patels, and up to the time of Peshwa Bajirao, they enjoyed the watan of
Sirdesai and Sirdeshpande, of the place, as will be seen, from the fol-
lowing letter, written by John Horn, Governor of Bombay, to Peshwa
Bajirao :—
"To   "BOMBAY CASTLE, 6th March 1734.
"The Illustrious Bajirao Pandit Pradhan, Prime Minister of the Most
Excellent Shahu Raja ; John Horn, President of India, Persia, and
Arabia, by the Most Illustrious English Company, Governor and Com-
mander-General of the Island and Castle of Bombay, and all its de-
pendencies ; By His Most Serene Majesty of Great Britain, whom
God preserve, sends him greeting,—I have received your letter of the
3rd instant in which you say that Antaji Raghunath, your servant, has
every claim to an Inam which from antiquity (his forefathers) had
enjoyed in the Portuguese territories granted by the ancient Emperors

The country contains fourteen parganas from the jurisdiction of Sáratbhate to the limit of Damaun.. At the same time, the office of Sirdesai and Sirdesh-- pande, was under the controlling power of Govind Mitkari. The abovementioned Mitkari lived for three years in the reign of Raja Bimbashah."[1] Now, we find from the early history of the Dekkan, that in the Shali-vahan *shaka* 1212, a Brahman of the Bháradwaja gotra, named Krishna, was in charge of the North Konkan as the Viceroy of the Devagiri King Rama-dev, and, therefore, it appears that "Karsan," from whom Raja Bimba took possession of the country of the Konkan, was identical with this Krishna.

It is stated that when King Bimbadev or Bimba--raja came to the island of Mahim (Bombay), he found that the place was occupied, mostly, by the Kolis and other lower castes. It was full of babul trees, and the only places of interest were the ancient shrines of Walukeshwar and Mumbadevi. The island was known by the name of Newale or Baradbet. The

---

of Hindustan, and afterwards confirmed by the kings of Portugal and continued by the Viceroys of Goa (in proof of which) he had several documents, but that the said Antaji Raghunath having been accused before the tribunal of the Inquisition craved your protection, and therefore you desire that the said documents be examined in our court of judi-cature, where if they are found to be true, an intimation may be made to the Portuguese to abide by what may be reasonable, to which I beg to reply :—That you are aware that the decision of such claims (suits) rests solely with the Government that granted the Inam, and that no other Government can interfere, and this being so it is useless for the said Antaji Raghunath to justify his claims in any tribunal, nay, for any Government to interfere with its authority or request, if the said Antaji Raghunath is accused before the Inquisition, over which Royal Authority itself has no power. I hope, you will command me in some other busi-ness in which I may be serviceable (to you). "

[1] *Vide* Appendix No. VI in Vaidya's Account of the Ancient Brahmans of North Konkan, p. 25.

king changed its name to Mahim or Mahikavati, caused fruit trees, and particularly cocoanut trees, to be planted there, and, built several temples, the principal one being that built in honour of his family deity Prabhawati or Prabhadevi.[1] He made Mahim, the capital of his kingdom, built there a palace for his own use,[2] and several mansions for the accommodation of the Rajas and Chiefs, who came to the Konkan, either with him, or after him, through the fear of the Moslems.

From a Danapatra or grant, of the rights of Sirdesai and Sirdeshpande, made, by King Bimbadev to his Raja-guru Purushottamrao Kavle, in the year *shaka* 1221 (A.D. 1299), we find, that the province of Konkan contained 14 parganas or districts, and 2 kasbas or sub-divisions, and that the island of Mahim (Bombay), was a pargana containing seven hamlets.[3] Accord-

---

[1] S. M. Nayak's History of the Prabhus, pp. 50—59.

[2] *Ibid.* At Mahim there is an oart which is still pointed out as the place where the palace of Bhimaraja stood, and where it is said old relics such as bricks, &c., are still found.

[3] The details are as follows :—

Taluka Malar		consisting of	57	villages.
„	Marol	„	57	„
Perganna Mahim (Bombay)		„	7	„
„	Uran Bhorgaon	„	9	„
„	Panch Nad	„	55	„
„	Khairan	„	45	„
„	Kaman Khanch	„	65	„
„	Sayban	„	84	„
„	Manori	„	84	„
„	Aseri	„	84	„
Kasba	Vasai	„	12	„
„	Sopara	„	16	„
Perganna Mahim		„	84	„
„	Mahab	„	27	„
„	Tarapur	„	364	„
Prant Sanje and Kamban		„	574	„

1,624

ing to this grant, in the month of Magh, *shaka* 1220
(A.D. 1298) Maharajadhiraja Bimbashah purchased
from Changunabai, widow of Govind Mitkari, the
watan of Sirdesai and Sirdeshpande of the provinces
of Malad, &c., for 24,000 rayals, and after keeping it,
in his possession, for one year and three months, pre-
sented it, as a religious gift, to his spiritual guide, Purushottamrao Kavle of the Bharadwaja gotra, on the
occasion of a solar eclipse, on the no-moon day of the
month of Vaishakha in the *shaka* year 1221 (A.D. 1299),
and in the presence of an assembly, consisting of
Prime Minister Mahadevrao Shrinivas, Chitnavis
Chandrabhan Parbhu, Patangrao Nyayadhish, and
other merchants, mahajans and jamindars.[1]

King Bhimadev died in the year *shaka* 1225 (A.D.
1303)[2] and was succeeded by his son Pratapbimba or
Pratapdev.

By some writers, it is believed, that, this Bimbadev
or Bhima Raja was identical with one of the Gujarat
Bhima Rajas of the Chalukya (Solanki) dynasty, who
reigned at Anahilwada; and Dr. DaCunha, (Origin of
Bombay, p. 39), observes that the Bhima Raja of
Gujarat, after his defeat by Mahomed of Guzni at
Somanath, in the year 1024 A.D., " fled from his coun-
try, and to make up for his loss in the north, marched

---

[1] The original of this Danapatra is now in the possession of the
descendants of the Raja-guru family of Malad, Thana District—*vide*
Vaidya's Account of the Ancient Brahmans of the North Konkan,
Appendix No. 8.

[2] *Vide* S. Nayak's History of the Prabhus, p. 59. This appears to be
a very short period for the improvements, &c., attributed to Bhima Raja.

with his colony from Patan into the south, and settled
at Mahim." Now, we know it as a historical fact,.
that immediately after the departure of Mahomed and
his army, Bhima Raja, again, returned to his country
of Anahilwada in Gujarat, caused the temple of
Somanath to be built of stones in place of the former·
wooden one, which was destroyed by Mahomed ; that a
few years later he sent an army against the Chief of
Abu, whom he subdued ; [1] and that he reigned at
Anahilwada till his death which happened in the year·
1064 A.D. [2]

The authors of Prabandha Chintamani and Dvyás-
raya (Jain Chronicles of Gujarat) have recorded, in
some cases, even the most minute details of the
reigns of the kings of the Chalukya dynasty of
Anahilwada, and had the conquest and colonization of
the Konkan or of Mahim by this Bhima Raja and his
Gujarat people, actually taken place, they would not
have omitted to chronicle so important an event.
At the time of Mahomed's invasion, the province of
the Konkan was under the sway of the Silaharas, and
from a copperplate grant dated *shaka* 948 (A.D. 1025)
we find that.the king, Chittaraj, was the ruler of the
1,400 Konkan villages, the chief of which were Puri
and Hanyaman, and, that the Taluka of *Shashasthi*
(Salsette) formed a part of his possessions. There is
no record of the province of the Konkan, being under

---

[1] *Bombay Gazetteer*, Vol. I, Part I, pp. 169-170.

[2] *Ibid*, p. 170.

the sovereignty of any one of the kings of the
Solanki dynasty of Gujarat, and the only king of that
house who successfully invaded the Konkan was
Kumarpal, who through his General, Ambada, defeated Mallikarjun, the Silahara king of the Konkan, in
A.D. 1160 ; but even then, the province does not appear
to have been annexed to the kingdom[1] of Anahilwada,
for we find that the Silaharas were the lords of the
Konkan till the year 1260 A.D., when the last Silahara king, Someshwar, was defeated and slain by
King Mahadev of Devagiri, and from that date, as
has been stated before, the sovereignty of the Konkan
passed from the hands of the Silaharas into those of the
Yadavas of Devagiri. Bhima Raja (II), who reigned
at Anahilwada from 1179 to 1242 A.D., was so weak,
that he was nicknamed *Bhola*, or the simpleton, and
the only thing the Gujarat chroniclers record about
him is, that, "his kingdom was gradually divided
among his powerful ministers and provincial chiefs."
It can, hardly, be expected, that so feeble a monarch,
could have accomplished the conquest of the Konkan,
which was, then, under the sway of the powerful Silahara kings, Aparaditya and his successor Keshidev.
Thus, it will be clearly perceived that there is very
little historical evidence to show, that Bhima Raja, who
settled at Mahim, was, a king of the Solanki dynasty
of Gujarat. On the other hand, it is an undisputed
historical fact that, during the thirteenth century of the

[1] Ind. Ant., V., p. 276.

3

Christian era, and more especially, at its close, the whole of the Northern Konkan, was under the sove-reignty of the Yadav Kings of Devagiri, and that the province was governed by Viceroys appointed from time to time, by Devagiri, kings. The last such Vice-roy was Krishna, of the Bharadwaj gotra (A.D. 1290), and evidently, Bhima Raja, the second son of King Ramadev, took possession and ownership of his father's dominions in the Konkan, from this man, in or about the year 1294 A.D., when Alla-ud-din invaded Deva-giri, and, defeated Ramadev and his son Shankardev. Among the Hindu princes, it was a custom, whenever a reigning king found that his life and kingdom were in danger, to send to a place of safety, a scion of the royal house in order that the royal *vansha*, or line, may not become extinct. And, it appears, that, follow-ing this ancient usage, King Ramadev, when he found that, he and his son Shankar, who had come to his aid, were surrounded by the Mogal army and were in danger of losing their lives and kingdom, must have taken the precaution of sending his son Bhimadev to the Konkan which was up to that time, free from the attacks of the Moslem invaders.

Mr. Murphy, in his " Remarks on the Oldest Races of Bombay," observes that the great influx of a variety of castes and races into Bombay, may be traced to certain events, which render the political and commercial history of the island a living record ; and that by studying their records, traditions, usages, origin, and meaning of the names of the localities, and especially their language, one may fairly come to certain conclusions regarding the history of this island and its dependencies, particularly Salsette." Let us, therefore, see what historical evidence or inference we can gather from the language, traditions, usage and records of the communities or castes, that came to Bombay, and colonized the island.

Four important communities or castes, *viz.* (1) the Patharé Prabhus and their priests, (2) the Palshikar Brahmans, (3) the Somavanshi-Kshatriyas or Panchakalshis, and (4) the Sheshavanshis or Bhandaris, are said to have come to Bombay with King Bhimadev, and these communities have played an important part in the early colonization and development of the island. The language spoken by these communities is Marathi, but the home language spoken by the Prabhus, Panchakalshis and Bhandaris, contains a large percentage of words borrowed from the aboriginal races of the island, the Kolis and Agris. The Palshikar Brahmans as religious guides and priests of these people, are socially and intellectually superior to them, and being in constant touch with religious Sanskrit literature, their home language does not contain so large a percentage of words, borrowed from the aboriginal races. Nevertheless, the language spoken by the oldest among their females, differs, widely, from the modern Marathi. In fact, it greatly resembles the language spoken in the

Dekkan in the 13th century of the Christian era, and
as such it would be a good test, for the purposes of in-
vestigation or research. Pick up from the *Dnyánesh-
wari* or similar other Marathi work of the 13th century,
five or ten words of pure Marathi origin, but, which
appear to be obsolete or out of use, and ask an unedu-
cated old lady of this Brahman community, whether
she understood any of them, and you will be surprised
to find that the old lady not only understands many of
these words, but, that she uses them, or at least used
them years before, in her conversation, and that it was
only the sneers of her educated daughter or daughter-
in-law, that made her relinquish their use. We give
below some such words, with their meaning in English, and their modern Marathi equivalents :—

	Old Marathi words.		Current Marathi words.		Meaning in English.
1.	*Tukne*	...	*Uchalne*	...	To raise up.
2.	*Surawad*	...	*Anukula*	...	Favourable.
3.	*Wokhaten*	...	*Waít*	...	Bad.
4.	*Chokhat*	...	*Shuddha*	...,	Pure.
5.	*Upég*	...	*Upayoga*	...	Use.
6.	*Thelen*	...	*Thévilén*	...	Placed.
7.	*Dekhane*	...	*Pahāne*	...	To see.
8.	*Latanken*	...	*Khoten*	...	False.
9.	*Dhavala*	...	*Pándhara*	...	White.
10.	*Udelen*	...	*Udayas alen*	...	Came to light.
11.	*Pokhala*	...	*Adarila*	...	Honoured.
12.	*Páik*	...	*Shipai* or *Chakar.*		Servant or sepoy.

From the above, it will be perceived that the language spoken by the highest of the communities that accompanied King Bhimadev, does not, much differ from the language that was in vogue in the Dekkan, at the time of the migration of Bhimadev and his followers to the Konkan, and the reason for this is obvious. The successors of Bhimadev, did not reign long in Bombay, for, we find that in the middle of the 14th century, the Moslem rule was firmly established in the island, which remained under their sway, till the advent of the Portuguese. And, after this, the people remained under the rule of the Portuguese, and subsequently of the English. Thus, they were, in fact, shut up from all intercourse with their castemen in the Dekkan, and consequently, their language had no scope for improvement or development, and remained very much similar to what it was, at the time of their migration.

The traditions of the Prabhus, Panchakalshis and their priests, the Palshikar Brahmans, are distinctly, in favour of the theory that they came from Paithan with King Bhimadev, the son of Ramadev, Raja of Devagiri, at the time when the town of Devagiri was invaded by Alla-ud-din, Emperor of Delhi ; and the old Maratha and Persian records, which are in the possession of some of them, tend to support this view.

King Bhimadev, as has been stated before, died in the year *shaka* 1225 (A.D. 1303), and was

succeeded by his son King Pratapbimb, also called
Pratapshah.[1]

· Nothing of importance is recorded or known about
him, except that he built another capital at Marol in
Salsette which he called Pratappur ; and, the name of
this capital is still preserved as Parjapur or Pardapur,
a deserted village, near the centre of Salsette.[2] It is
stated that Pratapshah was defeated and deprived of
his kingdom by Nagardev, Chief of Cheul ; and the
Mahomedan invaders of the Konkan, in their turn,
defeated the latter and deprived him of his dominions.[3]

In the year 1318, after the reduction of Devagiri and
the defeat and death of Harpaldev, son-in-law of the
Yadav King Ramadev, Mubarakh, the Emperor of
Delhi, ordered his garrisons to be extended as far as
the sea, and occupied Mahim and Salsette.[4] But,
Mahomedan supremacy does not appear to have been

---

[1] King Bhimadev was also called Bhimasbah or Bimbashah. In one
of the Persian records, in the possession of the Sirdesai family of Malad
it is stated that in the year *shaka* 1208 (?) Ramadev Raja with his son
Bhimadev went to pay his respects to Alla-ud-din at Delhi. He was
there very well received, and the king taking Bhimadev as his own son
conferred upon him the title of " Shah." It is true, that, Ramadev had
been to the court of Alla-ud-din, but the date given above does not appear to be correct: compare the following :—" Ramchandra was received
there (at Delhi) with great marks of favour and distinction, and royal
dignities were conferred upon him. And, not only was he restored to
his government, but other districts were added to his dominions, for all
of which, he did homage, and paid tribute to the King of Delhi. The
king, on this occasion, gave him the district of Nausari in Gujarat as a
personal estate and a hundred thousand tankas to pay his expenses
home."—*Bombay Gazetteer*, Vol. I, Part II, p. 532.
[2] *Bombay Gazetteer*, Vol. I, Part II, p. 26.
[3] *Bombay Gazetteer*, Vol. I, Part II, p. 27.
[4] Bombay Geo. Soc. Trans., Vol. V, p. 129.

firmly established, for from Marathi records we find
that King Pratapshah reigned for twenty-eight years,
i.e., till the year 1331, when he was killed and his kingdom usurped by his brother-in-law Nagardev, the Chief
of Cheul.[1]   Nagarshah reigned for 17 years, *i.e.*, till
the year 1347-48, when his dominions passed into the
hands of the Moslem rulers of Gujarat.[2]

According to Maratha accounts, the following causes
combined, to bring about the fall of King Nagardev.
The king had a favourite named Bhagadchuri. This
man was the son of one Jaitchuri, an illegitimate son
of the king. Bhagadchuri on being appointed by
Nagardev, Governor of the province of Sashti
(Salsette) greatly oppressed the inhabitants of that
place. He had the land measured, and divided it into
kathis, bighas, and haras ; and for each hara (= 8
bighas), the rayats were made to pay four maunds of
the produce of the land. Thus, revenue was raised
and royal favour gained ; and to the complaints
made against Bhagadchuri, Nagardev, on this account, paid no attention. Discontent was widespread,
for Bhagadchuri indulged his vicious propensities to
the full, outraged respectable women, and committed
more than one murder ; yet was permitted by the
king's favour to go unpunished.

The immediate cause of Nagardev's downfall, however, was the degradation by him, of one of his Sirdars,

---

[1] S. M. Naik's History of the Prabhus, p. 59-60.
[2] *Ibid.*

Nathrao Sindha Bhongle. Nathrao happened to dis-
please one Thakur Chaughale, a favourite of the king,
and was publicly disgraced. Burning with desire to be
revenged upon the king, Nathrao journeyed to Wad-
nagar interviewed the Sultan of that place, and urged
upon him the advisability of conquering the North
Konkan. The Sultan, therefore, ordered his General,
Nika Malik, to set forth. Nika Malik, taking an army
of 12,000 men, reached, by rapid marches, the Pargana
of Saiwan (Bassein Taluka ?), and there, encamped
near the Patalganga, in the forest of karvi trees.
Thence, he proceeded, by night, to the Kanheri Caves,
where he divided the army into three detachments.
One marched against Pratappur, the second against
Thana, and the third, under Nika Malik himself, invaded Mahim (Bombay). So sudden was the attack
that Nagardev, who had gone to Walukeshwar for
religious purposes, was quite unaware of the danger.
The defence of the royal palace, therefore, devolved
upon his queen, and a few retainers, and in the
struggle the queen was slain, and the palace looted.
By this time, a message had reached Nagardev, who,
gathering his men together, marched back to meet
the Moslem forces. A battle ensued at Bhayakhala
(Byculla), in which Nagardev was defeated and
slain ; and thus came to an end the sovereignty of the
Hindu kings over the island of Bombay and its
dependencies.

CHAPTER II.

OBSERVATIONS ON THE GROWTH OF POPULATION AND THE CONDITION OF THE PEOPLE, &c., UNDER THE HINDU RULERS.

EXCEPT the Buddistic relics found at Elephanta, the Mauryas do not appear to have left, any visible traces of their supremacy, over the island of Bombay. The kings of the Maurya dynasty were very zealous patrons of the faith of Gautama Buddha, and the town of Puri was the capital of their kingdom. Although there is a diversity of views regarding the site of Puri, there is a consensus of opinion, in favour of the theory, that, the site of this remarkable city, must be traced to the north-east portion of the island of Elephanta or Gharapuri, where ancient relics have been discovered. In fact, it is clear from the writings of the early Portuguese travellers, that, up to the middle of the Sixteenth Century of the Christian era, the island of Elephanta was known by the name of Puri, and that the names of Elephanta and Gharapuri are of later origin. Garcia da Orta[1] who visited it in 1534 A.D. says :—" There is another pagoda better than all

---

[1] Dr. Cunha's " Origin of Bombay," p. 26.

4

others in an island called " Pori," and we name it
the island of Elephant. There is a hill on it, and at
the top of this hill, an underground dwelling, hewn
out of a living rock. This dwelling is as large as a
monastery, and has open courts, and cisterns of very
good water. On the walls around, there are very large
sculptured images of elephants, lions, tigers, and of
many human figures well represented. It is a thing
worth seeing, and it seems that the devil put there all
his strength and skill, to deceive the heathens, with
his worship. At present, this pagoda is much damaged
by the cattle that enter its inside, and in the year thirty-
four when 1 came from Portugal it was really worth
seeing." Another Portuguese writer, Simao Botelho,
records that "the island of Pori, which is of the
elephant, was rented (in 1548) to Joao Pirez, by per-
mission from the Governor, Joao de Castro, for one
hundred and five pardaos."

Puri was a town of such great importance and
opulence that it was called *Lakshmi*, or the goddess of
fortune of the western ocean. Its wealth and mari-
time greatness attracted the attention, and excited the
envy, of the neighbouring rajas, and in the beginning of
the Seventh Century, King Pulakeshi of the Chalukya
dynasty, invaded it, with hundreds of ships, and captured it, from the hands of the Mauryas. The Chalu-
kyas, have not left, any ostensible relic of their rule,
except perhaps the surnames of " Chalke " and
"Salunke." But, the Silaharas, who succeeded them

and ruled from 810-1260 A.D., have left many marks
and traces indicating the high degree of civilization
and prosperity attained by them. As has been stated
before, Puri was the capital of their kingdom, and it
was called by them *Shatanandapuri*, or " the city of a
hundred pleasures," and *Mangalpuri*, or " the city
of prosperity." The interesting sculptured figures of
the Elephanta Caves, are the lasting monuments of the
power and glory of the Silaharas. The scenery of
the Bombay harbour is, by itself, most picturesque
and attractive ; but, it must be admitted that the
wondrous and picturesque scenes of the Elephanta
Caves, give a special charm to the attractive and
picturesque sights of Bombay harbour, and enhance
its grandeur and glory.

The Silaharas of the Northern Konkan carried the
Suvarna Garuda, i.e., the figure of a golden eagle, on
their royal standard, and instead of a separate crest we
generally find the figure of a *Garuda* also on the seals
of their copperplate grants. They gloried in the
hereditary title of *Tagarapura-Parameshwara*, or the
supreme lord of the town of Tagarapura. The exact
site of this Tagarapura has not yet been identified ;
Dr. Burgess identifies it with Roza near Daulatabad,
Wilford with Devagiri, Bhagwanlal with Junnar, Dr.
Bhandarkar with Dharur, and Dr. Fleet with Kara-
vira or Kolhapur. The Silaharas were staunch
Shaivites. They built numerous temples of the
god Shiv in the Konkan, and it is believed that the

ancient shrine of Walukeshwar[1] which was situated at Malabar Point, was built by the Silaharas. This belief is strengthened by the fact that the sacred *Yoni* at the old Walukeshwar Temple (through which people used to pass to prove their unblemished character), was called *Shri-gundi*, a word of Kanarese origin. The Silaharas are said to be southerners or of Dravidian origin, and it appears from their copperplate grants, that, Ayyas or Dravidian Hindus had a considerable influence at their courts. In the grants, we come across such names as Naglayya, Lakshmanayya, Anantpai Prabhu, Belala Prabhu and Peramde Pandit. The Prabhus referred to here, are most probably, the ancestors of the Kayasth Prabhus of the Konkan. Large districts were called *rashtras*, subdivisions were called *vishayas*, the villages *gramas*, and the village headmen *pattakila*, the modern patil. They had a king's high road called *Rajapath* passing a little north of Bhandup and following the same line as the present road from Bombay to Thana.[2]

In the year 1260, the supremacy of the Silaharas over the Konkan, came to an end, and with the decline of their power, the town of Puri merged into insignificance. The Yadavas, who succeeded the Silaharas, governed the Konkan through their Viceroys, whose

---

[1] The remains at Walukeshwar consist of about 60 richly carved stones, pillar capital, statues and other temple fragments, one of them about 6'×3', apparently of the 10th century, which lies near the present Walukeshwar temple on Malabar Point.

[2] *Bombay Gazeteer*, Vol. I, Part II, p. 21.

head-quarters were either at Bassein or *Shristhanak*
Thana, and, it is not, till the advent of Bhimaraja
or Bimbdev about the year 1294 A.D. to the Konkan,
that we hear of Bombay or rather "Mumbai-Mahim"
and its neighbourhood. In fact, it is from the date of
the advent of Bhimadev, that the real history of the
colonization and growth of Bombay begins. Enough
has already been said about the identity of this
Bhima Raja, and about the races that accompanied
him, and settled in and about the island of Bombay.
In addition to the four important communities, *viz.*, the
Palshikar Brahmans, the Prabhus, the Somavanshis
and the Sheshavanshis or Bhongle Bhandaris, that
came with Bhimadev, another caste of Bombay
Hindus, the Agris, claim allegiance to Bhimadev, and
state that they came to Bombay from Mungi Paithan
with Bhima Raja, the son of Ramadev. Most of
these castes, at one time or another, enjoyed special
privileges[1] in Bombay, and many of them own landed
properties even to this day.

---

[1] It will be seen from the patent granted by John Wyborne that the
descendants of the Brahman followers of Bhimaraja continued to enjoy
certain privileges also under the British rule :—
"Whereas Kashinath Gamba Naique, Withal Naique and Bana
Paddia, of Mahim, Brahmins, have for this many years past granted the
office of Brahmins in the township of Mahim and its jurisdictions in performing the rites and ceremonies of marriage, administering physique
to the sick and doing and performing all other ceremonies relating to
the said office, as appears to me by several orders, I have thought fit
and do hereby order you, the said Kashinath Naique, Withal Naique and
Bana Paddia, do continue in the said office of Brahmins giving full
power to act in the same and to perform all the rites and ceremonies of
marriage and to administer physique to the said inhabitants of the town
of Mahim, and its jurisdictions, prohibiting all persons whatsoever from
molesting or disturbing you in the execution of the said office upon any

Bhima Raja was the real benefactor of Bombay, for, it was he, who, charmed with the position and scenery of the island, first conceived the idea, of colonizing it, and gave a practical shape to his idea by building, palaces and houses, by planting cocoanut and other garden trees, and by making it the capital of his kingdom.

According to a local tradition prevalent among the descendants of the followers of Bhima Raja, it is stated that he had two palaces in Bombay, one at Kheda (Lower Mahim), and the other (which was the principal seat of Nyaya or justice) was at Naigaon on the spot where the 'Arshe Mahal,' or Mirror Palace, of Jivanlal Maharaj stands. This place is still known in the village as Bhima Raja's Wadi. Close by, were assigned quarters for the *Raja-guru*, or royal preceptor, and other Brahman followers, and the place came to be called Brahman Ali, or Bamanoli, *i.e.*, the street of Brahmans. The Agri followers had three divisions among them, *viz.*, Thakurs, Bhoirs, and Govads. The Thakurs were petty officers in the army, and the place

pretence whatsoever. Given under my hand and sealed with the seal of the Court of Judicature of the island of Bombay, this 22nd of August Anno Domini 1685.

(Sd.) J. VAUSE.

I do hereby confirm and ratify Kashinath, &c., Brahmins, in their office in ordering all the respective inhabitants of Mahim to pay a dutiful respect suitable to their employes.

Bombay, this 29th October, 1686.

(Sd.) STEPHEN COLT, (Sd.) JOHN WYBORNE.
Secretary.

Upon the request of the within named persons this is confirmed upon them.

Bombay Castle, 22nd June, 1889. (Sd.) J. CHILD."

Note.—The original of the above is at present in the joint possession of Chintaman Balambhat Naik and Nilkanth Vithal Paddhe, hereditary priests of Mahim.

where they settled, came to be called Thakurwady.
The Bhoirs were the palanquin bearers, and the
locality they settled in, came to be called Bhoirwady,
or Bhoiwady, as it is now called. The Prabhus settled
in the proximity of their temple of Prabhadevi, while
the Somavanshis or Panchakalshis had their colony at
Parel. Here, they built three temples under the pa-
tronage of the Raja, two for their family deities,
Wageshwari and Chandika, and the third for Mahadev,
and called it *Parali Vaijanath Mahadev*. It is said
that the *ling* of this Mahadev is *Swayambhu* or inar-
tificial, and, therefore, it was considered of equal importance in sanctity, as the celebrated *ling* of *Vaijanath*
at Parali, in the Dekkan. And as the Mahadev was
called Vaijanath Mahadev, the village came to be
called Parali or Paral. The temple of this Mahadev
is, at present, situated in the middle of the Parel
village, and is said to be on the same spot, where
the old temple stood.

The good old people of Bombay have not forgotten
Bhima Raja, the benefactor of this island. He is
deified and worshipped by the villagers. In the oart
called the Bhima Raja's oart or *Arshe Mahal*, he is
represented by a black stone besmeared with red paint
and flowers, and the descendants of his followers,
especially the old Bhoirs and Thakurs, make homage
to this stone, by worshipping it with flowers, milk,
clarified butter, &c., and offering not only fruits,
but also goats and fowls. Till recently, an annual

jatra or fair used to be held in his honour, when animals were sacrificed ; but the new Maharaja owner of this oart, being a strict Vaishnav, has put a stop to this, and he has advised the people to feed Brahmans (instead of offering animal sacrifices), for the pacification of the spirit of Bhima Raja, who is said to haunt, or as the people say, keep a watch over the place of his past glory.

APPENDIX A.

NOTE ON THE DERIVATION OF THE WORD BOMBAY.

OPINIONS differ about the origin and significance of the word Bombay. By some writers, it is believed, that the name Bombay is derived from two Portuguese words *bom*, good, and *bahia*, bay or harbour, and that the Portuguese gave this name to the island on account of its excellent harbour. But, according to the rules of euphony, the correct combination of *bom* and *bahia* would be "Boa-bahia," and not "Bom-bahia," (bahia being of the feminine gender), and had the Portuguese given the name "Bombaim" to the island on account of its good harbour, they would have, certainly, called it "Boa-bahia." But what do we find? We find that most of the Portuguese writers speak of the island as "Bombaim," and that in the papers relating to the grant of the island of Bombay as part of the marriage-dowry, by the King of Portugal to King Charles II. of England, the word "Bom-baim" is used.

Another explanation given about the origin of the word Bombay is, that it is derived from the word Mubárak,[1] the name of a Mahomedan King, who is supposed

---

[1] Brigg's Ferista I., p. 306.

to have held sway over the island of Bombay. There is a
probability of truth in this belief, and let us see how far it is
borne out by historical evidence and local traditions. From
the Maratha records published and unpublished, and from
other sources, we find that up to the end of the thirteenth
century the greater part of the Northern Konkan, including
the islands of Bombay (Mahim) and Salsette (Shristhan),
was at one time or other, under the rule of the Hindu kings
of the Silahar dynasty, and the Yadavas of Devagiri. About
the beginning of the fourteenth century, i.e., in the year
1318 A.D., after the reduction of Devagiri, and the death of
Harpaldev, the son-in-law of Ramadev Rane, the last sovereign of the Yadava dynasty, Emperor Mubarak I. ordered his
garrisons to be extended as far as the sea, and in obedience
to his directions, the islands of Mahim and Salsette were
occupied by his forces.[1]   From the above, it is plain that
in the fourteenth century, Mahim (Bombay) and Salsette,
were brought under the rule of Emperor Mubarak I. of
Delhi. But, there is nothing on record to show, that the
Emperor gave his name to the island, and had this island
been called Mubarakpur or Mubarakabad, after the Emperor Mubarak, Mahomedan historians of the subsequent
period would have made use of that name in referring to
the conquest of the island, instead of calling it by the
name of Mahim (Bombay), as will be shown hereafter.
According to Briggs (Ferista II., 413), in the year 1429
A.D., Malik-ul-Tujar, a General of the Bahamani King of
the Dekkan, led a large army into the Konkan, brought
the whole country under subjection, and took several

---

[1] Brigg's Ferista I., 373; Bombay Geo. Sty.'s Trans V., 129.

elephants and cart-loads of gold and silver, as booty
to his master, the Bahamani King. Malik-ul-Tujar
then seized on Mahim (Bombay) and Salsette. The
seizure of these two islands aroused the wrath of Ahmed
Shah,[1] the King of Gujarat, to such an extent that he immediately sent a large army to recapture these important
places. A part of this army went by land, and a part
embarked in seventeen ships. And this combined army
laid siege to Thana, by sea and land. Malik-ul-Tujar
offered some resistance to this force, but, eventually, he
abandoned the place, and returned to Mahim, where·it
appears a part of his army was stationed. Having strengthened his forces by additional reinforcement at Mahim
(Bombay), Malik-ul-Tujar returned to Thana. Here, he
attacked the combined forces of Ahmed Shah. A bloody
engagement took place between the two forces, and it is
stated, it lasted a whole day. The army of Malik-ul-Tujar
was completely defeated and dispersed ; and the fleet
of Ahmed Shah returned to Gujarat, carrying with it some
beautiful gold and silver embroidered muslins, taken on
the island of Mahim[2] (Bombay). The above account is
corroborated by Erskine[3], who states that Ahmed Shah
during his reign, reduced under his power, the Northern
Konkan and the island of Bombay. In the Mirat-i-Ahmedi,
a list is given of the possessions of the Gujarat King
Mahamad Shah Begada (who died in 1511 A.D.), and
these are made to include, in the Konkan, the districts

---

[1] Forbes' Ras Mala I., 350.

[2] Brigg's Ferista IV., 29 ; Forbes' Ras Mala, 350-351.

[3] Erskine's History of Gujarat, 110.

of Bassein, Mahim (Bombay), Daman and Danda Rajapur[1] (Janjira).

From this account, and the authorities given above, it is conclusively proved that (1) in the fourteenth and the fifteenth centuries of the Christian era, the Northern Konkan including the island of Bombay, was under the sway of the Mahomedan Kings (for the most part, if not exclusively) of Gujarat; (2) that during the whole of this period the island of Bombay was known by the name of Mahim and not as Bombay or Mubarakpur; (3) and that it (Mahim) was a place of some importance, politically and commercially.

According to a local tradition which is based on the authority of a work called *Mumba Devi Mahatmya or Puran*, the name Mumba is given in the memory of a monster named Mumbarakh, who was supreme in this island. We have got a copy of this so-called *Puran* with us. It is written in Sanskrit, and contains fifty-two verses in the *anushtup* metre, or nearly 208 lines. It states that a long time ago, there lived on the island of Bombay, a powerful Daitya (monster). He was a great devotee of the god Brahma, whom he pleased by his strict performance of religious austerities, for a number of years. At last, the god Brahma was pleased with him, and informed him that he would be glad to grant him any boon that he may ask for. The monster thanked the god, and requested him to grant him such a boon, that by virtue of it, he would be invincible in battles, and would not suffer death at the hands of man, gods, yakshas, gandharvas, demons, animals, serpents,

---

[1] Bird's History of Gujarat, 110.

beasts and birds. The god Brahma granted this boon immediately, and from that day, Mumbarakh began to harass everybody on earth. The people on earth, therefore, went to Vishnu, the god of protection. As it was owing to the favour of the god Brahma that the demon Mumbarakh had become invincible, god Vishnu went to Brahma, and in his company they all went to Kailas, the residence of the god Shiva (the Hindu god of destruction). Vishnu informed Shiva of the havoc, created by the demon Mumbarakh. Shiva was greatly enraged, and in his anger, he threw out from his mouth a part of his *tej* or lustre, and commanded all the gods to do likewise. And from the combined *tej* or lustre of all the gods a female deity was created. All the gods now implored her to protect them from the demon. The goddess consented, and came to the nether world. On seeing the goddess the demon Mumbarakh came to attack her, seated in a chariot. Upon this the goddess invoked her *vahan* (vehicle) the lion, and the lion of the goddess Amba at once appeared before her. Riding on this lion, Mumbadevi fought with the demon for eight days, at the end of which the demon was vanquished, and he prayed for mercy. He praised the goddess and she was pleased. He promised not to harass any one in future, and to go to *Patal* (the lower regions), provided the goddess adopted his name before her name, and stayed in the island. The goddess consented, and it is stated that from that time she adopted the name of Mumbadevi, and stayed in the island.

In conclusion, the writer of this Puran says, " those who want health, wealth and prosperity, and those who want victory on the battlefield, power of oratory, succession of progeny, &c., should worship this goddess with flowers, fruits, and presents of money, ornaments and jewels, and they should also feed Brahmans and give them good *dakshina* or money presents. Evidently, the author of this Puran was a Brahman priest, fond of money presents (dakshina), and he must have been a half-educated Brahman, for the verses are full of grammatical inaccuracies, and here and there we find an utter disregard to the rules of Sanskrit prosody. But, this is not all. At the end of this Puran, the writer gives a very interesting and amusing piece of information. He states, "Having heard of the prowess of the goddess from Rama, the great warrior (monkey god) Hanuman, came to Bombay, immediately, and has been ever since staying in this island." The author of this Puran further tells us that, "In order to strengthen the defences of this island against any encroachment, the goddess Mumba commanded one hundred thousand of her *Ganas* or fighting followers to come and settle in Bombay."[1]

There is no doubt that the City of Bombay derives its name from the goddess Mumba. But the question is how is the word Mumba derived? Is it a foreign word? Or is it the name of a Hindu goddess? Two explanations seem plausible, and they are (1) that the name Mumba is derived from Munga or Muga, the name of a *Koli* fisherman, or (2) that it is derived from the

---

[1] भुत्वा क्षेत्रस्य महात्म्यं । हनुमानपि राघवात् ।
स्थितो मुम्बापुरे नित्यं । भक्ताभिष्टप्रदोहरिः ॥ 49 ॥
तथान्ये क्षेत्ररक्षार्थं ! देव्या व्यापारिताः शुभा ॥
गणाश्शत सहस्रंवा । मुंबापुर्यां व्यवस्थिताः ॥ 50 ॥

name of Amba Bhawani, a Hindu goddess. Let us examine these two explanations, and see which of them is worthy of credence and acceptance. By some authorities, it is firmly believed that the word is derived from Munga or Muga, the name of the Koli who first built the temple of the goddess Mumbadevi. But, we generally find that whenever any Hindu deities are called after the name of the builder of the temple, the name of the male builder is given to the god and of the female builder, or of the male builder's wife, is given to the goddess. The feminine of the word Munga is Mungi, and therefore, the correct form would have been Mungi-ai and not Munga-ai or Mumba-ai. Another explanation of the origin of the word Mumba is, that it is derived from Amba; another name of Bhawani[1], the consort of Shiva (the Hindu god of destruction) ; and in our opinion this latter explanation is correct. As the goddess Káli is sometimes called Mahákáli or the great Kali, so Amba is also called Maha Amba or the great Amba, and by the Kolis and other illiterate persons the word Maha-Amba is generally pronounced as Mamba or Mumba. The suffix *Ai* signifying mother is a term of respect applied to Hindu goddesses. The word Mumbai is, therefore, derived from the words Maha + Amba + Ai = Mumbai ; and evidently the word Bombay (Portuguese *Bombaim*) is the corruption of the word Mumbai.

---

[1] Bhawani is often called Amba, Ambika or Ambálika. Compare the following Sanskrit prayer in the Ganpati Atharwa Shirsha : अंबे अंबिके अंबालिके नमः &c. *i.e.,* I bow to thee O Amba ! O Ambika ! O Ambalika !

Many instances can be given of names of towns and villages being similarly derived, *i.e.*, from the names of the local deities. We shall, here, give only three such instances. Take Wasai, the name by which the town of Bassein is called by the natives of the place. This town takes its name of Wasai, from the name of the goddess Watsa or Watsala, and Watsa + ai = Watsai or Wasai. Again take the name Gorai, a village in Salsette. It is derived from Gauri + ai. Gauri is the name of the goddess Bhawani, and by the villagers she is called Gaur or Gor. The name Jogái (Jagaiche Ambe), is similarly derived. Joga is the diminutive of the word Jogeshwari (the name of a well-known goddess), and the word Jogài is derived from Joga + ai, meaning the goddess mother Joga.

APPENDIX B.

(The following was published in the TIMES OF INDIA *of 16th April 1902.)*

THE STORY OF SALSETTE.

INTERESTING RELICS FOUND.

In the " Hindu Period " of Mr. S. M. Edwardes' " History of Bombay," it is stated that Pratapdev, the son and successor of the celebrated Bhima Raja of Bombay, changed his capital, or rather founded a new capital in the centre of Salsette, and called it Pratappur, after his own name. Sir James Campbell, in Volume XIV of the *Bombay Gasetteer*, opines that the probable site of this Pratappur might be found in the deserted village of Parjapur in Salsette ; and those interested were therefore anxious to see if any important archæological remains or traces of the old city, could be discovered in this deserted village. For this purpose, during the last Christmas holidays, two investigators went to Marol and thence proceeded to Parjapur. This village is, at present, in the possession of Mr. H. A. Wadia, of Bombay, being granted to his ancestors by Government in 1808, in exchange for a site near the Apollo Pier gate. After much careful inquiry and search, the party came across several raised sites called by the villagers of Marol "Gharthàns." These Gharthàns were carefully examined and excavations

were carried on at different places. The result of this has
been that three images of Hindu goddesses were discovered buried under ground. These have been dug out, and
placed in a conspicuous part of the village. Traces were
also found of six Hindu temples, and an equal number
of ponds. Pieces of well-dressed and carved stones
and stone pillars, were also discovered. Further excavations were directed to be carried out at different places in
the village, and from reports recently received, we learn
that the foundations of a large number of houses of well-
dressed stone, have been discovered. It is believed that if
excavation on a larger scale be carried out, further and
more important relics may be discovered.

According to Maratha accounts Pratapdev changed his
capital from Mahim (Bombay) to Pratappur, owing to the
invasion of Bombay by the forces of the Mahomedan
Emperor of Delhi. From Brigg's "Ferista" we learn
that in the year 1318 A.D., after the reduction of Devagiri and the defeat and death of Harpaldeo, the son-in-
law of the Monarch of Devagiri, the Emperor Mubarak
ordered his garrisons to be extended to the seas, and occupied Mahim (Bombay). It appears that it was probably
about this time that King Pratapdev thought seriously of
securing for himself and family a place of safety in times of
danger, and with this object, he founded the city of Pratappur in the centre of Salsette. The site, no doubt, was
very charming, and in truth it is still so ; for at the
distance of only a few hundred yards lie the interesting
caves of Vihárávali and the charming hills of Vihárávali
and Kondivti, and close by is situated the village of Pas-

pavli (Palsavli) which also contains old relics, and which, according to the Bhimbakhyan, Bhima Raja granted as a religious gift to his Rajguru. There is a local tradition that the town and temples of Parjapur were destroyed and desecrated by the Portuguese, and traces of this desecration are still visible, for among the ruins of a Hindu temple were discovered pieces of broken crosses. The dilapidated walls of a Portuguese Church built on the foundation of a Hindu temple are distinctly visible.

The enquirers in question have also been able to discover in Salsette two ancient stone slabs containing inscriptions in Sanskrit. The larger of these stone slabs measures 8 by 3 feet, and contains the figures of the sun and the moon, and the ass curse. The characters are Devanagari, and the language is Sanskrit, with an intermixture of Prakrit words. They are supposed to relate to lands granted by the Silahara kings of Salsette. We understand that these are now being deciphered by Mr. A. M. T. Jackson, M.A., I.C.S., who since the demise of Drs. Inderji and Paterson, is the only scholar in Bombay able to do full justice to this subject. The result of Mr. Jackson's readings of the inscriptions will be awaited with interest.

APPENDIX C.

(The following was published in the TIMES OF INDIA *of 19th April 1902.)*

THE STORY OF BOMBAY.

SOME UNREGARDED ANTIQUITIES.

WITH reference to the account that appeared in the *Times of India* of the 16th instant, regarding the discovery of interesting archæological remains in Salsette, I beg to state that in addition to the two stone slabs referred to therein, we have been able to obtain, with the help of the Mamlatdar of the place, a third stone slab containing an interesting inscription in Sanskrit. It bears the date *Samvat* 1389, corresponding to the year 1333 A.D., and purports to commemorate the building of a temple and well by Nagradev (Nagardev ?). But who is this Nagradev ? In the chapter on the Hindu period contributed to Mr· Edwardes' "History of Bombay" it is stated at page 16, on the authority of Marathi papers, that Pratapdeo (who was also called Pratapsha) died in the year 1331 A. D., and was succeeded by his brother-in-law Nagardev of Chaul. The inscription in question bears the date 1389 *Samvat*, and, therefore, it appears that the event, which the inscription commemorates, happened in the third or fourth year of Nagardev's reign. Unhappily, the stone is a broken half, and until the other half of it is obtained, no definite conclusion can be arrived at regarding the identity of this

Nagradev. This stone slab was found in a well in the premises of Rao Saheb Ravji V. Shunkershett at Ghod Bander ; and if the Rao Saheb will help us in finding out the other half, he will be doing a great service to the cause of the early history of Bombay and Salsette.

To students of ancient history and archæology the island of Salsette affords a vast field for research, notwithstanding the fact that Sir James Campbell, Mr. Mullock and the late Dr. Indrajee have searched and noted down every object and place of interest in the island. Besides Parjapur and Paspavli, there are many other places of antiquarian interest, such as Malad, Juhu, Pahadi, Borivli, &c., in Salsette. Some years ago, at the behest of Sir James Campbell, I visited Juhu and Malad in the company of a descendant of the Rajaguru Kavle, and at Juhu we found in a cocoanut oart, traces of Buddhistic relics. But nearer home in the crowded city of Bombay, and its suburbs, there are and were objects which, though worth noticing, we have hitherto neglected. A few paces from the Government House, Parel, lies the temple of the *Swayambhu* Mahadev, the sanctity of which was considered as great as that of the Parali Vaijanath, and which is supposed to give its name to the district of Parel. And a few yards further, is situated the historical temple of Wageshwari, a name which affords some scope for philological investigations, or, to use your own expression, " philological speculations." What these are I reserve for a future communication. On the other side of the Government House, *i.e.*, the Bhoiwada Gate side, and not at a very long distance, lies the site of the ancient palace of Bhima Raja, called the

"Bhimraja's Wady," and here the descendants of Bhima Raja's followers, still cherish the memory of the King by worshipping a black stone representing the Raja, and by offering to it fruits and fowls, at certain seasons of the year.

About a few hundred yards from the Bhima Raja's Wady, lies the oart of the hereditary priest of Mahim, who is a descendant of Bhima Raja's Brahman followers, and who holds patents granted to his ancestors by Governors like R. Bourchier, Sir John Child and Sir John Wyborne (1685), confirming the "rights and privileges of presiding at the religious ceremonies of the Gentoos of the island and of administering physique (medicine)." In the rear of this oart, there stands half buried in the compound wall, an old stone slab called the Bhima Raja's *Dan Shila.* The inscription is almost obliterated. In the year 1887 the celebrated Dr. Darmestetter of Paris visited this place with me for the purpose of deciphering the inscription, and for inspecting the patents and Sanskrit and vernacular manuscripts of antiquarian interest. I believe the late Dr. Darmestetter refers to this visit in his "Lettres sur l'Inde." And last year, this place was visited by a noble English lady[1] of high rank and of philanthropic tendencies, on a mission of charity. Among the papers preserved here, are some interesting original letters from Bajirav Peshva and his brother Chimnaji Appa to Antaji Raghunath Kavle Rajaguru, concerting measures for the capture of Salsette from the hands of the Portuguese.

---

[1] This distinguished lady was no other than the wife of the present popular Governor of Bombay.

Only a few months ago, while collecting some unpublished writings of the poet Namdev from the archives of a Hindu Temple in Bombay, I was informed by the *pujari* that a few years ago he had seen in a *chameli* field at Sewri two *Palias* commonly called by the villagers *Bhima Rajache hathiche pai*, *i.e.*, the feet of Bhima Raja's elephants. The *Palias* are memorial stones about four or five feet in length and eighteen to twenty inches in breadth, and used to be erected in the memory of some great chief killed in battle. As the information was confirmed by several other trustworthy persons, I made diligent enquiries but without success ; and now I learn that these Palia stones were removed or destroyed by the owners of stone quarries. If the above information is correct, what a pity it is that such a ruthless desecration of ancient monuments, should have been perpetrated in the very heart of this most enlightened island city, and withal, at no long distance from the palace of the rulers of the Western Presidency.

BOMBAY, *April 17th.*   P. B. JOSHI.

Lightning Source UK Ltd.
Milton Keynes UK
UKHW021049180219
337526UK00006B/844/P